AF815622

Python Programming for Beginners!

Step-by-Step Learning Guide

By

Gary D. Anderson

Python Programming for Beginners!
Step-by-Step Learning Guide

ISBN: 978-1-7364232-2-6

Contents

Contents

Why Learn Python: Unlocking Possibilities

In the world of programming, Python has become the coding tool of choice for countless types of applications. It is recognized as one of the most versatile, accessible, and popular coding methods in use today. Its appeal extends from seasoned developers to coding novices for many compelling reasons, making it a language of choice for millions around the globe. So, why learn Python?

Simplicity and Readability:

Python's hallmark is its straightforward and readable syntax. Unlike some other programming languages with complex structures and symbols, Python employs a style of coding that is clean and intuitive. Its indentation-based block structure enforces good coding practices, promoting code clarity and reduces the likelihood of errors. This simplicity makes Python an excellent starting point for anyone who wants to learn coding.

Versatility:

Python has proven itself in terms of its versatility, and is widely accepted and used within many different business and industrial applications. Whether you're programming for automation, data analysis, web development, or delving into the world of artificial intelligence, Python can handle practically any task with relative ease.

Abundance of Resources:

The Python community is large and active. A global collective of developers continually contributes to its growth and refinement. This type of community support translates into a vast ecosystem of resources that serve as building blocks for projects, and can dramatically reduce development time and facilitate the rapid creation of applications that support all types of projects.

Built-in Functionality:

Python's extensive standard library is composed of pre-built code modules and packages. This built-in functionality covers a broad spectrum of tasks, such as extended math functions, the handling of data structures and manipulating files, and performing network operations. With Python, the tools are in place that allow developers to focus on solving problems - rather than reinventing the wheel.

Cross-Platform Performance:

Python's cross-platform compatibility is another asset that enhances its popularity. Whether you're using Windows, macOS, Linux, or virtually any other operating system, Python code can be deployed without significant modifications. This versatility ensures that Python projects are highly portable, enabling them to run across different environments. All things considered, whether you're just starting your journey into programming or seeking to enhance your existing skill set, Python is a valuable and user-friendly tool for creative programming solutions.

Installing & Using Python:

In learning and using Python, we'll employ the use of chapter objectives, together with the repetition of concepts and functions used in the previous lessons. In this way, you will build your repertoire of skills as we progress from simple concepts, to those that are more difficult. I believe Python is relatively easy to learn and fun to use, so after each basic lesson objective is satisfied, I encourage you to turn your imagination and creativity loose, experimenting with different aspects of the coding exercise.

Python IDE: Installation & Use:

For the basic step-by-step coding lessons shown throughout this book, there are some different options for you to download the Python development platform. One option is simply to download the free Python IDE (version 3.12 series). It includes a development platform (IDE) called IDLE, which is very simple and straight-forward to use. A second option, and I think the best, is to download *VS Code* from the link shown below. It is easy to install and use, and if you download and install the recommended extensions, gives you a very versatile programming environment. In any case, you'll need to download Python, as shown under option 1, then the VS Code download.

Option 1: Download IDLE, Python's Integrated Development Platform

Go to: "***python.org/downloads***" and download the version necessary for your operating system, I downloaded and use the version for Windows 10, both the "Embedded 64-bit" files and the "Windows Installer". Once installed, you can open and use IDLE, which is Python's Integrated Development and Learning Environment (IDE).

IDLE has the following features:

- It is coded in 100% pure Python.
- Works on Windows, Unix, and macOS.
- Utilizes a shell window (interactive interpreter) with colorizing of code input, output, and error messages.
- Multi-window text editor with undo, Python colorizing, smart indent, call tips, auto completion, and other features.
- Debugger with persistent breakpoints, stepping, and viewing of global and local namespaces.

Here are a couple of screen shots showing the interactive Shell and Editor windows. Note that the "Run" and "Run Module" options are available under the "Run" tab of the Editor window, where code is entered. Program output, once the code is executed, will be shown in the Shell window.

When IDLE is first started, the *Shell window* opens. From the Shell window, you can open existing python code modules or create new by selecting the options from the dropdown menu of the File tab.

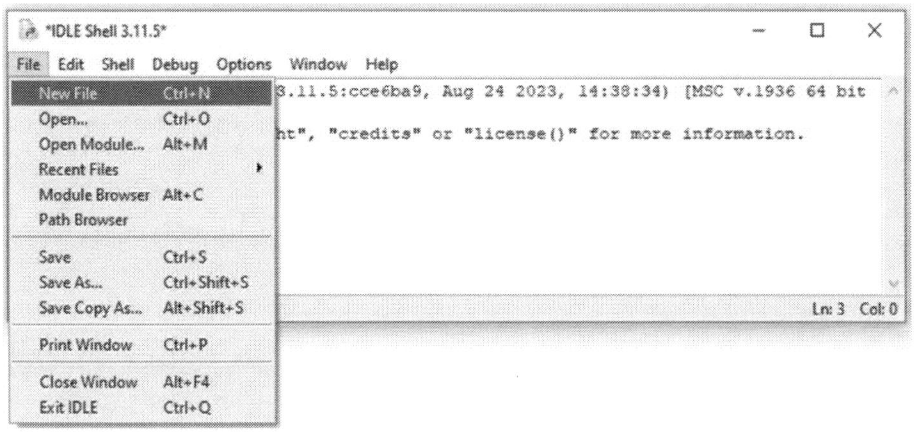

Both the Shell and Editor windows have menu selections allowing you to create a new or open an existing python (.py) file. For instance; if you have used a text editor, such as notepad, to write a program. You can then rename the program to change the file extension from ".txt" to the ".py" extension used in python programs. Then, simply "open" the program file in the IDLE Shell or Editor window "file" tab.

In either case; "*open existing*" or *"create new*", the *Editor window* opens where you can enter code for a new program, run your code, perform testing and additional editing as necessary. Also, by selecting the "Options" tab, you can tell IDLE to open in the *Editor* window upon start-up, as shown below. With this window open you can immediately begin to enter code.

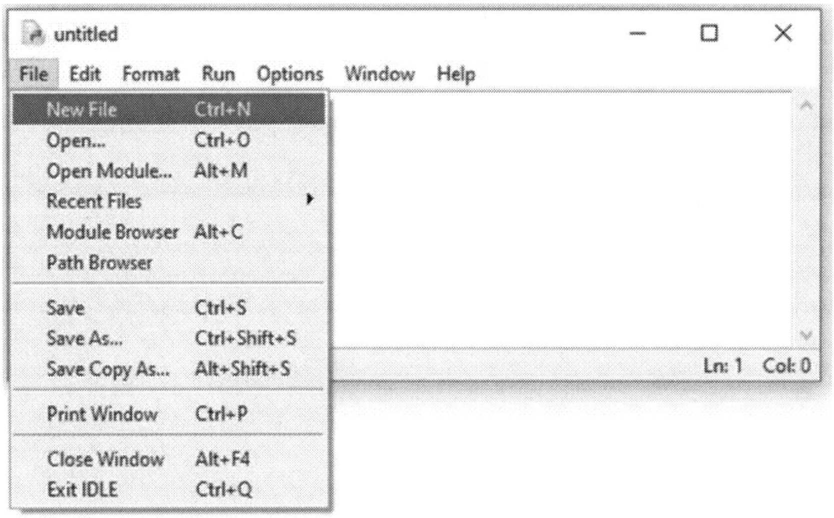

This is perhaps the quickest option for getting Python up and going, and is an easy-to-use programming environment, although you'll do quite a bit of switching between the Shell and Editor windows.

Option 2: Download and use VS Code

Another way of programming in Python, and my preference, is through the use of Visual Studio Code. Download *VS Code* and install. After installation and opening *VS Code*, I was prompted to install the VS Code Extension, which adds some additional features to the platform. I recommend going through the familiarization walk-through, which helps with some program setup. Here you can designate the folder where your programs will be stored and retrieved.

- Step 1: Download and install VS Code. Here is the website:

  https://code.visualstudio.com/download

Final Note:

As you get started on the following lesson topics, here are some things to consider.

- First of all; this book initially focuses on very basic and fundamental programming concepts, using simple examples and lesson objectives. The goal of course, is to become proficient in the use of coding techniques – where certain things become second nature. The objectives and examples shown throughout this short book, are geared for those who are just beginning to program and exploring the possibilities of Python. The goal is to provide a foundation to build upon as you expand your coding skills.

- That said, any and all of the material covered here can be researched online, or through the tutorials and reference libraries included with your Python downloads. As mentioned earlier, Python has a large and active online community which greatly enhances the learning environment and experience. If there is a task you want to accomplish using Python, but are unsure about the "how-to-do" on the coding, be assured that someone has probably developed a way to do it, and presented it online.

- In each chapter, I encourage you to enter and run the sample code snippets and programs, - just as shown. After doing that, take some time getting creative with the coding and lesson objectives. Try different methods of accomplishing the same task. Just have some fun with the coding, make some mistakes, and see what works and what doesn't. Pay particular attention to any syntax errors or messages you get whenever your program doesn't run as desired. These messages often will show the specific line of code where the problem exists, and give you feedback on solving the problem.

Lesson 1: The Print Function

In this lesson we'll begin with a look into Python's *print function,* which outputs a string variable directly to the computer screen. In the lessons and examples that follow, we'll explore the concepts of concatenation, the use of escape characters to add lines and tabs, and also the means of adding variables of different *datatypes* to the printed output. But for now, let's just focus on the basic *print function*, which outputs a word or phrase to the computer screen.

Create the program shown below that simply prints "**Hello World**!" to your screen as output. Enter these lines of code into either the IDLE editor window or the VS Code, save the program and then "run" the module to see your output.

Sample Code:

```
# Print a simple string variable
print("Hello World!")
```

Notes & Observations:

- The variable "Hello World", shown in the print statement, is a *string variable.*
- String datatypes are always designated by the use of quotation marks, either "*double-quotes*" or '*single-quotes'*. By using both types of quotation symbols, you can also use conjunctions containing a single quote, within a single string variable.
- A string variable can also include "spaces", "numbers", and "special characters".
- Note the use of the hashtag "#" to designate a *comment* within the program code. Comments are "non-executable" lines used to add descriptive content to your program.

- Printing the string variable "Hello World!" to the console screen, is accomplished by using the *print( ) function.* This only one of Python's many resident or "*built-in*" functions.

Lesson 2: Concatenation with Strings

This lesson makes use of the print function, to output a variable directly to the computer screen. By using the "+" symbol within the print instruction, multiple variables, in this case all string variables, can be added to the print output. The is referred to as "*concatenation*". Explore both the print function and concatenation techniques in performing the lesson objective that follows.

Create the simple program shown below, putting your name into the "*your-name*" field. Once you run the program, the output prints to screen the "Welcome" sentence and includes your name. As the comments show, the object of this exercise is to get you thinking about the readability of your output, and methods of adding spaces in appropriate places. Explore ways to create spacing, making output more readable.

Here are three variations that alter spacing in our programs output.

Sample Code:

```
# this will print without spaces!
print("Welcome to our class" + "your-name")

# this will add a space between class and name!
print("Welcome to our class " + "your-name")

# this will also add a space to the printed output!
print("Welcome to our class" + " " + "your-name")
```

Notes & Observations:

- Start lines of code at the beginning of the line without indentation.
- Note the use of quotation marks that define what is inside the parenthesis as a string variable. Single quotes can be used as well.

- Use the "+" symbol, *not within quotes*, to concatenate variables.
- Integrate spaces *within* the quotations to make a program output more readable.

Lesson 3: The Input Function & Variable Assignment

In this lesson you will use the *input function* to obtain user-information. As the user enters their response, that information can be reassigned to a variable, making it easier to use in other parts of the program.

Objectives:

Create the programs shown that queries for specific user response, reassigns those responses to other variables, then concatenates them into a single line of print. Using the *concatenation* technique shown in the previous lesson, join variables together within the print statement. Integrate the escape characters "\n" and "\t" to make the user input more readable as it is output to the screen.

Sample Code:

```
# Examine the input function & assignment to a variable
pet = input("What is the name of your favorite pet? ")
print("hello " + pet)
```

Sample Code:

```
# Fruit Salad
print("Let's list two of your favorite fruits!")
name = input("Hello, what is your name?\t")
fruit_1 = input("What is your favorite fruit? \n")
fruit_2 = input("What is your 2nd favorite fruit? \n")
print("So "+ name + ", your favorite fruits are " + fruit_1 + " & " + fruit_2 + ".")
```

Notes & Observations:

- Note that when a string is assigned a variable name, that name can be placed directly into a print statement *without the use of quotations*.

- Naming variables follow certain rules:
    a. No spaces allowed, but the use of the underscore is permitted. Therefore: the name “fruit_2” is allowed, while “fruit 2” is not.
    b. Can’t start with a number, and can’t use special characters.
    c. Avoid the use of reserved keywords that reference python functions.

- Input strings are placed into the *designated* variables, for example: my_number, name, client_name, fruit_1, and fruit_2. These variables are *containers* for the user response, which is a string. They could also hold a number, such as an integer or float value, but *would still be treated as a string value.* If in our example; numbers are entered into the fruit_1 and fruit_2 variables, math operations are not possible until these are converted to a numeric datatype. This is referred to as “casting”.

- The “+” symbol is used to concatenate different string variables.

- Note the usage of *escape sequence* characters, such as the “\n”, which moves the cursor to the *next line* to await an input value, and the use of the “\t” combination, *which tabs the cursor to the right* and awaits the input value. These escape sequence characters must also be placed within your quotation marks.

Lesson 4: Len & Type Functions

Create and run the program shown below that explores the use of Python's *length* and *type* functions.

- Using the *length* (len) instruction will return the length of a *string* variable.
- Using the *type* instruction, will return the *data-type* of any variable.
- Continue to use the *input* and *assignment* techniques used previously.

We'll look more into different datatypes in the next lesson or so, but for now simply note that "12345" is a string variable because it is within quotes; while 12345 (no quotes), would be considered an *integer* value of 12,345. So, as you can see, there are times when you'll need to know a variable "type" before using it in further program operations.

Sample Code:

```
# Return the Length and Type of an input string.

name = input("To get started, what is your name? ")
print("This is the length and variable type of your name.")
print(len(name))
print(type(name))

# Show differences in how Python handles string and integer datatypes.

print("The first example is an integer, the second a string, the last an integer.")
print(123456)           # Prints an integer value
print("123" + "456")    # Prints two strings using concatenation.
print(123 + 456)        # Performs a Math operation and prints the result.
```

Notes & Observations:

- In the first sample code, note the assignment of the input to the variable "name".
- The *len* function is only used on strings, *not on integer or float variables.*
- The *len* function *returns an integer value.*
- The *type* function can be used to check any variable datatype.

On the lines of code that use the *len* and *type* functions, consider the *order of steps performed within the program line.* Python steps from the inner-most parenthesis to the outer-most; taking the string contained within the variable "name", performing the length (len) or type (type) function, and finally *prints* the result as an output to the screen.

Sample Code:

```
# Checking different variable datatypes and length.

print(type("abc"))
print(type(123))
print(type(3.14))
print(type(True))
name_of_user = input("Enter your name: ")
length_of_name = len(name_of_user)
print(type(name_of_user))                # Shows the variable is a string.
print(type(length_of_name))              # Shows the variable is an integer.

# Two methods of printing results of "Length of your name".
# One method using concatenation and conversion of integer to string.
# Another method adding multiple datatypes to a single print statement the "f-string" method.
print("The number of letters in your name: " + str(length_of_name))
print(f"The number of letters in your name: {length_of_name}")

# Note the use of the curly-braces { } around the variable, and the leading "f" within the
parenthesis. This is commonly referred to as the "f-string" method, and allows you to include
different datatypes within the print function.
```

Lesson 5: Datatypes & Conversion

Create and run the example programs that use the *type* function to verify different datatypes. Perform conversions for changing strings into integer or float datatypes, and back when necessary.

Here are some of the most basic datatypes used:

- String (str): Any ordered sequence of characters, (“Hello World!”), (“12,345”).
- Integer (int): Whole numbers, (2, 5, 16, -3)
- Float (f): Numbers with a decimal place. (3.146, or 0.003)
- Boolean (bool): Logical value of “True” or “False”

Here are a few examples of *string* variables – designated by the use of double, single, and triple quotes. Try this code sample, and experiment with your own variations. Note the usage of (\n) for creating a blank line, the (\t) for a tab, and also the use of the *triple quote* for entering a *multi-line string.*

Sample Code:

```
### String variables and the use of quotation marks.

sample_1 = "This is a typical string variable using double quotes!"
sample_2 = ‘A string can also be designated by single quotes!'
sample_3 = 'Quotes can be used within a string; for example, “I want to learn Python!" '
sample_4 = """Use triple-quotes for a longer, multi-line string.  Also, a string can be shown as a
numeric value, such as +/- 9999.999, but must be 'cast' as an integer or float variable before it
could be used in a math operation."""

print(sample_1)
print(sample_2)
print(sample_3)
print(sample_4)
```

Next shown is a sample program that receives a value into an input string variable, does a check to verify its type, and then converts it (casting) into a numeric value. In this form it can be utilized in math calculations.

Sample Code:

```
### Variable conversion, using types string & integer
two_digit_number = input("Enter any two-digit number: ")

# Show the datatype of "two_digit_number"

print("This verifies that our 'two_digit_number' is actually a string: ")
print(type("two_digit_number"))
# Convert this string to an integer, and reassign it to "my_number"
my_number = int(two_digit_number)
print("This verifies that 'my_number' is now an integer value.")
print(type(my_number))

# Perform some Math
print("Math operations can now be performed using our two-digit number.")
my_number = (my_number * 2)
print("The two-digit number multiplied by 2 is equal to: " + str(my_number))
```

Notes & Observations:

- Consider again, the order of steps performed by the Python program line containing multiple functions: stepping from *inside to out*, taking the variable "two_digit_number", a string variable, then performing the *type* function, and finally the print function, which results as output to the screen.

- The variable "*two_digit_number*" is converted into an integer, then put into "*my_number*", and its *type* is checked and verified as output to screen.

- Note that I've shown assignment to a different variable name in this example, but the int( ) function could be performed on the variable "*two_digit_number*" and put into the *same* variable name if so desired.

- Observe that in the final print statement, we had to convert the variable "my_number" into a string. In the next examples you'll learn how mixed variable types can be put into a single print function.

In the previous code sample, and in the one that follows, the program converts a string into a different datatype. It then adds the numbers and converts the float result back into a string to be used within a print statement.

Sample Code:

```
### Floating point conversion and add two floating point values
f_number1 = input("Enter a floating point number: ")
f_number2 = input("Enter a 2nd floating point number: ")
# Convert each string to a numeric value (float) and add the numbers.
result = float(f_number1) + float(f_number2)
# Print the resulting floating-point value.
print(result)
# Print the result again by converting back into a string, then concatenate for print string.
print("These numbers add to: " + str(result) + " once converted to float values!")
```

Notes & Observations:

- Conversion is shown here as a separate step, but can also be performed directly from the input instruction lines. Here is an example:

```
f_number = float(input("Enter a floating point number."))
```

- Integer or float variables <u>*will not concatenate*</u> into the above print string without conversion back into a string. Therefore; the "+ str(result) +" is required in the final "print" function of the program shown above.

- Examples that follow will use the "f-string" technique, which allows the integration of *different datatypes* into a single print statement. Here's an example of using the *f-string method* to print mixed variables, a string variable and a floating-point number.

```
print(f"These numbers add to: {result}, once converted to float values!")
```

Sample Code / Using conversion *and* the f-string method.

```
### Floating point conversion and add two floating point values.
f_number1 = input("Enter a floating point number: ")
f_number2 = input("Enter a 2nd floating point number: ")

# Convert these strings to numeric values (float) and add the numbers.
result = float(f_number1) + float(f_number2)
print(result)

# Print using concatenate of string datatypes.
print ("These numbers add to: " + str(result) + " once converted to float values!")

# Print using the f-string method and mixed datatypes.
print (f"The numbers entered add to: {result}, a floating-point value!")
```

Notes & Observations:

- Use of the character "f" at the *beginning of the string – outside of the quotes.*
- The use of curly-braces { } around the float variable name, and the absence of the "+" symbols normally used for concatenation.
- The fact that the float variable is placed *within* the longer string variable quotes.

Lesson 6: Slicing & Indexing

Slicing and indexing are two programming concepts commonly used in Python. Until now, we've only considered the fundamental datatypes; such as the *string,* the *integer*, the *float* and *Boolean.* Now it's time to consider other important datatypes used in Python, such as the *list* and *tuple.* Slicing and indexing are the means used to access specific elements in a sequence, which can be a string, a list, a tuple or one of the other sequence datatypes that follow.

In these sequence examples, note the differences in how data items or elements are enclosed; some use parenthesis, while others use curly-braces, or brackets. Also consider the de-limiters used for item separation, such as the colon or comma. When it comes to the actual entries into a sequence, the same naming conventions apply for strings, integers, or float values. In this section we'll focus mainly upon *lists* and *tuples*, which are data structures Python uses to store collections of items. The key difference between lists and tuples are that lists are "mutable", which simply means you can modify the contents by adding, removing or editing the elements of the list. Conversely; once a tuple is created, it is "immutable", meaning the contents can't be changed. Therefore; lists are used in scenarios where you need to add or modify data, and tuples used in scenarios where you want to ensure data security – as in database records.

As you can see in the descriptions shown; list items are separated by commas, and enclosed by *square-brackets*. Contents of a tuple are separated by a comma, and enclosed by *parenthesis*. Indexing and slicing of lists and tuples are performed in the same way, using 0-based indexing, and this will be the focus of this chapter. *Set* and *Dict* datatypes are used to hold *unordered* and *ordered* collections of data, and are not accessed in the same way.

- List: Ordered, *mutable* sequence. [12, “hello”, 2023]
- Tuples (tup): Ordered, *immutable* sequence of objects: (12, “hello”, 135.66)
- Sets: (set): Unordered collection of unique objects: {“a”, “b”}
- Dict: Ordered pairs. {“emp_num”: “value”, “name”: “Fred”}

By using the *indexing* and *slicing* techniques the follow, you can extract characters from a string, list, or tuple. Understanding how to use slicing and indexing is essential for working with data in Python, so let's explore these concepts, and provide some examples to help you better understand how they work.

Indexing:

Indexing is the process of accessing an individual element in a sequence by referencing its *position* in the sequence, referred to as its index. In Python, indexing starts at 0 (the *leftmost* position), or the first element of the sequence, the second element is at position 1, and so on. To access any element of the sequence, simply use square brackets [ ] with the index number of the element you want to access. Here is a short block of code that uses indexing to *pull specific characters from a string*, *convert them to integers*, and then performs a simple math operation using these numbers.

Sample Code: # Convert strings and add the first and last digits of a three digit string.

```
three_digit_number = input("Enter any number having 3 or more digits! ")
result = int(three_digit_number[0]) + int(three_digit_number[2])
print(result)
```

Here is another example of indexing that accesses a *List,* which is an "ordered sequence" that uses brackets, and items separated by comma. Index positions start counting from *left-to-right* are: [0,1,2,3,4]. In this code, we have created a list, called "fruit_list", and used indexing to access the second and fourth elements in the list using their respective indices. Remember that the leftmost element is the [0] index position

Sample Code:

```
fruit_list = ["apple", "peach", "orange", "banana", "plum"]
print(fruit_list[1])          # Output will be "peach".
print(fruit_list[4])          # Output will be "plum".
```

Note that elements *can also* be referenced from *right-to-left* using *negative index values* as shown in this example: [-5, -4, -3, -2, -1]. Therefore; negative indexing can be used on *fruit_list*, to reference and use the identical sequence element from a list. Using the same list of fruit and negative indexing we obtain the following output results.

```
print(fruit_list[-4])      # Output: "peach".
print(fruit_list[-1])      # Output: "plum".
print(fruit_list[0])       # Output: "apple".
print(fruit_list[-5])      # Output: "apple".
print(fruit_list[1])       # Output: "peach".
print(fruit_list[-4])      # Output: "peach".
print(fruit_list[-1])      # Output: "plum".
print(fruit_list[-2])      # Output: "banana".
print(fruit_list[3])       # Output: "banana".
print(fruit_list[2])       # Output: "orange".
print(fruit_list[-3])      # Output: "orange".
```

Slicing:

Slicing is the process of accessing a *section of sequence elements* by specifying the *starting* and *ending* index positions. A *step* position is optional but sometimes necessary to pull selected data, and defaults to 1 if left out of the function. In Python, slicing is performed on a list (or other sequence), by designating start and end indices, separated by a colon. The syntax for slicing is shown on the following examples. Note that the "end" index value is *non-inclusive* of the position entered, and that the *step* position usage is optional.

- *Sequence_name*[start : end]
- *Sequence_name*[start : end : step]

Here are examples showing different slices taken from "fruit_list". Enter these snippets of code and run, which should result in the outputs shown below. Take some time to experiment with different indices, both positive and negative, and examine the differences created in your output.

Sample Code: Slicing using *positive* indices.

```
## print[start: stop: step] Positive Indices
fruit_list = ["apple", "peach", "orange", "banana", "plum"]
print(fruit_list[1 : 4])      # Output: peach, orange, banana
print(fruit_list[0 : 4 : 2])  # Output: apple, orange
print(fruit_list[1 : 4 : 2])  # Output: peach, banana
```

Sample Code: Slicing using *negative* indices.

```
##print[start: stop: step] Using negative indices
fruit_list = ["apple", "peach", "orange", "banana", "plum"]
print(fruit_list[-5:-1:1])  # Output: apple, peach, orange, banana
print(fruit_list[-2:])      # Output: banana, plum (Last two items)
print(fruit_list[:-3:-1])   # Output: plum, banana (Last two items reversed)
```

Notes & Observations:

- Indexing and slicing techniques are used in Python to extract data from larger sequences. These sequences can be *lists, tuples, dict* or *set* sequences, or a single *string*.

- You may have had your fill of fruit for the time being, but here are some additional methods of slicing not shown in the above examples. These are instances in which the numeric position value is not shown, - only the colon separators. Anywhere a number isn't shown within the slice, *default values* are used. The defaults for (*start:end:step*), are zero (0), the entire list (array), and one (1). This is shown on the first two examples; either of which will return the entire list.

Examples using *(start:end:step)* indexing:

```
fruit_list = ["apple", "peach", "orange", "banana", "plum"]
(fruit_list [0:])  # apple, peach, orange, banana, plum # (returns entire array)
(fruit_list[:])    # apple, peach, orange, banana, plum # (returns entire array)
(fruit_list[:4])   # apple, peach, orange, banana # (end -1, not inclusive of end)
(fruit_list[-3:])  # orange, banana, plum #  (start is -3 item and returns last 3)
(fruit_list[:-3])  # apple, peach (returns everything except the last 3 items)
(fruit_list[::-1])   # plum, banana, orange, peach, apple (all items, reversed)
```

The "Set" Datatype:

As stated earlier, *sets* are "unordered" collections of unique elements, and are not accessed by conventional indexing methods. These examples are worth some time spent learning to access and manipulate the data items contained in sets.

```
# Using the following Sets
set1 = {1, 2, 3, 4, 5, 5, 3, 6, 7, 8, 9, 2, 10}
set2 = {1, 3, 5, "John", "Jane", 10, 12, 15}

# Check for Membership in a Set
print("John" in set1)  # Output is "False"
print("John" in set2)  # Output is "True"

# Check for Membership in a Set, by using the "If / in" keywords
if "Jane" in set2:
  print("Jane is in this group!")
else:
  print("Jane is not found.")

# Remove Duplicate values in a Set
set3 = set(set1)
print(set3)                    # Output for set3 = {1, 2, 3, 4, 5, 6, 7, 8, 9, 10}

# Print all items in a set using the "for / in" keywords
for item in set2:
  print(item)

# Adding an item to a "Set"
set2.add("Andy")
print("Set2 now holds the following items: ", set2)

# Adding items of Set2 to Set1, and remove duplicates
set1.update(set2)
set1 = set(set1)
print("This is the new 'set1': ", set1)
```

The "Dict" Datatype:

A "Dict" or *dictionary,* starting with Python 3.7, is now an "ordered" collection of *key-value* pairs. In addition to being ordered, it is also mutable (changeable) and doesn't allow duplicate items. You access a *dict value* by referencing its associated *key*, as in the following examples:

```
# Samples of "dict" access & use #

name_age = {"name1": "Gary", "age": 52, "name2": "Jan", "age2": 43}

print(name_age["name2"])
print(name_age["age2"])
# Output will be:
        Jan
        43

# Adding and deleting information in a "dict" datatype #
emp_info = {"name": "Andrew", "emp_num": 1324501, "age": 32}  # Employee data

emp_info["email"] = "andrew@example.net"   # Add an item to dict, Assign value
print(emp_info)                    # Print the revised with new content
del emp_info["age"]                  # Remove 'age' from the content
print(emp_info)                    # Print the revised contents

# Print output of "emp_info" will show:
{'name': 'Andrew', 'emp_num': 1324501, 'age': 32, 'email': 'andrew@example.net'}
{'name': 'Andrew', 'emp_num': 1324501, 'email': 'andrew@example.net'}

# Remove an item from the "dict" contents using the ".pop()" method.
emp_info.pop("email")  # Remove the specified value #
print(emp_info)

# Printed output will be:
{'name': 'Andrew', 'emp_num': 1324501}
```

- Using syntax "*dict.pop(arg)*": removes the specified argument (a key).
- Using syntax "*dict.pop()*" : removes the last item from the dict datatype.

Lesson 7: Math Operations

Math operations follow the PEMDAS rule, in the order of operations performed by any type of math computation. Therefore, math operations will follow the order shown here:

1. *Items within Parenthesis*: Items within inner most parenthesis performed first.
2. *Items raised to an Exponent*: The operator for exponents is the "**" double-asterisk.
3. *Multiplication & Division*: Use the single-asterisk "*" to multiply, and the " / " for division.
4. *Addition & Subtraction*: Using the "+" for addition, and for subtraction the " - " symbol.
5. *Left-to-right order on operations*: Operations with equal priorities will calculate from left to right.

Here are some examples, but key-in and test your own variations in exploring how Python follows the PEMDAS order of operations. These show many of the built-in math functions of Python, but additional functions are available by using Python's math module. Note that these math operations can be entered directly into the IDLE Shell window. When the [Enter] key is pressed, the line is executed and the result shown. This makes it convenient for testing the results of an equation or function.

```
3 + 3 * 6               #Output: 21

(3 + 3) * 6             #Output: 36

3 + 3 * 6 ** 2          #Output: 111     Use the double asterisk to apply an exponent.

3 + (3 * 6) ** 2        #Output: 327

5 + 6 – 1 / 2 ** 3      #Output: 10.875

(5 + 6 – 1) / 2 ** 3    #Output: 1.25
```

```
round (3.499)          #Output: 3

round (3.500)          #Output: 4

round (3.499, 2)       #Output: 3.49

pow (3, 4)             #Output: 81        For pow (x, y), "x" is raised to "y" power.

abs (-12.541)          #Output: 12.541 Returns the positive absolute value.

min (4, 6, 19, 3, 2)   #Output: 2 Returns the minimum of the set.

max (4, 6, 19, 3, 2)   #Output: 19 Returns the maximum of the set.

11 % 3                 #Output: 2, The "modulo" (%) returns the remainder of the division operation.
                        Therefore: 11 divided by 3 returns 2.
```

Objectives:

Create and run this code that calculates *body mass index* (BMI). Make sure you understand each step the program takes in its execution, including the math operations and the order they are performed. In this example, I've used some conversion factors to obtain the metric values. Also, note the use of the *f-string technique* on the printed result.

Sample Code:

```
### BMI Calculator ###

height = float(input("enter your height in feet: "))
weight = float(input("enter your weight in pounds: "))

height_m = height / 3.3            #convert to meters
weight_kg = weight / 2.205         #convert to kilograms
BMI = weight_kg/height_m**2 #calculate BMI
BMI = (int(round(BMI)))            #make it a rounded integer
print(f"Your BMI is: {BMI}")       #print the resultant BMI
```

The next example is a short program that uses many of the functions and techniques we've covered thus far. Once again, these include math operations, variable assignment, and datatype conversions. Conversions are for both float and integer values. The printed output will be the *total cost of the bill plus a tip*, and the *cost per person when splitting the bill.*

Sample Code:

```
### TIP Calculator ###

print("Welcome to the tip calculator!\n")
total_bill = float(input("Enter the bill amount: $"))
Tip = int(input("Enter percentage for a tip: (e.g., 12, 15, or 18?) "))
Split_num = int(input("How many people are splitting the bill? "))
Tot_per = ((total_bill * (1 + (Tip/100))) / Split_num)
Tot_per = round(Tot_per, 2)
Bill_total = total_bill * (1 + (Tip/100))
Bill_total = round(Bill_total, 2)
print(f"The total bill with tip is: ${Bill_total}.")
print(f"The total cost per person, including tip would be: ${Tot_per}")
```

Formatting for Floating-Point Values:

In this code block, we've used a rounding function, along with the *second argument* which specifies the *number of decimal places* to round the floating-point values. This works pretty well for many applications; however, you'll find that if the second precision decimal place happens to be a zero (0), then it will be dropped from the output when using the "*round(a, b)*" function. Run this code module using 100 for the bill, giving a 10% tip, and splitting the bill between 2 or 4 people. As you will see, the calculated output result of $27.5 will show as the *total cost per person*. So, while this rounding method may be used, it may not be acceptable for the desired output if you are wanting to show currency having two decimal points, as in this scenario of calculating a tip amount per person. Fortunately, there are other means of formatting in this type of situation. Shown next, are two additional methods of accomplishing the same decimal formatting, and a brief description of the elements used. Substitute the following code lines in place of the rounding code, lines 8 and 10, and test for different results.

```
Tot_per = "{:.2f}".format(Tot_per)
Bill_total = "{:.2f}".format(Bill_total)
```

In Python programming, the `{:.2f}` format is often used to control the formatting of floating-point numbers when they are displayed as strings. Here's what each part of `{:.2f}` means:

- The curly braces "{ }"are used as *placeholders for values* that you want inserted into a string.

- The colon ":" is used to *indicate that you are entering a format specification* for the value that will be inserted into the placeholder.

- The entry of “.2f “is the *format specification* and consists of two parts:

  1. The dot or “period is used to indicate that you are formatting the value's precision (decimal places).

  2. The `2f` specifies that you want to format the value as a floating-point number with 2 decimal places. Change the value for the desired number of decimal places.

Here are two additional examples showing these basic methods of using the `{:.2f}` in Python code:

```
# Using the str.format() method

value = 3.14159
value = "{:.2f}".format(value)
print(value)                        # Output: 3.14


# Using f-String method

value = 2.71828
value = f"{value:.2f}"
print(formatted_value)              # Output: 2.72
```

In both of these examples, the floating-point numbers `3.14159` and `2.71828` are formatted using the method syntax of “{:.2f}”, allowing them to be displayed with only 2 decimal places. This method works well anytime you need to establish the exact precision of floating-point values for readability. But as shown in the earlier example; sometimes a simple rounding function will accomplish exactly what you need.

Here is the Tip-Calculator program integrating these different formatting instructions:

Sample Code:

```
print("Welcome to the Tip Calculator!")
total_bill = float(input("What was the total bill?  $ "))
tip = int(input("What percentage tip would you like to give? 10 12 15 percent:  "))
people = int(input("How many people to split the bill? "))
total_with = (total_bill*((tip/bill)+1))
each = (total_bill*((tip/bill)+1))/people

# Include special formatting for two decimal places with our currency values.

total_with = "{:.2f}".format(total_with)
each = f"{each:.2f}"
bill = f"{bill:.2f}"
# Print output for selected variables
print(f"Each person's split would be: $ {each}")
print(f"The total bill before tip is: ${total_bill}")
print(f"You have chosen to tip {tip} percent")
print(f"The total bill with tip is $ {total_with}, and split is $ {each} per person.")
```

As I close this section on math operations and functions, I want to bring to your attention the usage of the additional *modules* provided within Python. These modules *expand the capabilities* of your code by providing additional tools and functions.

Next is an example that uses some of the *Math Module* functions that are available, such as the *sqrt(x)* function. Take the time to run this and play with different aspects of this code. For instance, in the previous code used to calculate BMI, I used the "**" to square a value in the calculation, but I could also have used the math function *pow(x, y)*.

Explore different rounding options, and different options for making output more "readable". Most importantly, ensure you understand what each line is doing.

Here is a sample code block that shows example usage of various math module functions.

```
# Examples of Math Module Functions
import math                                     # Import the Math Module
# Using the following variables
number = 18
decimal_val = 4.68
angle_deg = 30

# Perform the following math functions:
sqrt_result = math.sqrt(number)                 # take the square-root of number:
exp_result = math.pow(number, 3)                # number raised to the power of:
angle_radians = math.radians(angle_deg)         # convert degrees to radians:
sin_result = math.sin(angle_radians)            # what is the sine of angle_radians
cos_result = math.cos(angle_radians)            # what is the cosine of angle_radians:
pi_val = math.pi                                # returns the value of pi:
e_val = math.e                                  # returns the value of euler's number:
floor_result = math.floor(decimal_val)          # returns the floor value (next lowest
integer):
ceil_result = math.ceil(decimal_val)            # returns the ceiling value (next highest int):

# Display results of these math functions
print()
print(f"Square root of {number}: is {sqrt_result}\n")
print(f"{number} raised to the power of 3 is {exp_result}\n")
print(f"Sine of {angle_deg}: is {sin_result}\n")
print(f"Cosine of {angle_deg}: is {cos_result}\n")
print(f"The value of 'Pi' is:  {pi_val}\n")
print(f"The value of 'Eulers number' is:  {e_val}\n")
print(f"Floor of {decimal_val} is: {floor_result}\n")
print(f"Ceiling of {decimal_val} is: {ceil_result}\n")
```

Finally, as we move into the next section on "Flow Control". It is important to be aware of the difference in the usage of the *equal* character when programming your code. At this point we've frequently used the equal sign (=) to assign a string, integer or float value to a variable. I always think of a variable as a simply a container to hold something. That *something* may change as the program progresses from beginning to end. With that said; the equal symbol is quite important in the world of programming, so let's examine three different ways it is commonly used in Python.

- The single "=" sign is used to *assign* something to a variable name. Therefore, we see code lines such as these:

```
sqr_val = (int(my_number) ** 2)

value = 3.14159
```

- The double "==" is used for *comparisons,* and so is used in portions of code where *conditional comparisons* are needed.

```
if my-number == 25:
  Then do this
Else:
  Do this
```

- The *augmented assignment operator* that enables a variable to be "augmented" by a simple math operation. An example of this might be:

my_num += 5   Adds 5 to *my_num* each time the instruction is executed.

my_num *2   Multiplies *my_num* by 2 on each execution of the code.

More will be shown on using comparison symbols in the next chapter as we look into typical methods of program flow control.

Lesson 8: Flow Control

In this lesson, we take a look into the use of "if" functions to control the flow of our executed code. The goal is to use instructions based on meeting specific conditions, and eliminating or "bypassing" other options if those conditions are not met. This is accomplished by using the "if" function, along with its *variants:* the "if/else" and "if/elif" combinations, to test for acceptable conditions. When using comparison operators for program flow control, the following symbols and conventions apply:

- *Equal:* (==)
- *Not-equal*: (! =)
- *Less than*: (<)
- *Less than or Equal*: (<=)
- *Greater than*: (>)
- *Greater than or Equal:* (>=)

Here are some examples that use these comparison operations within the "if" function variants. The first example is acceptable and works properly. Also shown are two examples that *create an error* due to the *improper use* of the equal (==) symbol.

- The single equal symbol "=" assigns a value to a variable. The value can be an integer, float, or string type of data. The named variable is a container that holds the value.

- The double equal combination, "==" is used to compare expressions or variables for equality, and thus is used for testing conditions.

- Exceptions are the permissible use of a single equal symbol in combination with the *greater than* (>) or the *less than* (<) symbols. Therefore the (>=) or the (<=)

key combinations are allowed in comparison functions, and are shown in some following examples.

Here are some examples illustrating usage of comparisons and conditions tested by using "if" instructions. As noted, the last two examples of code will generate errors.

```
### Basic "if" with correct usage of assignment and comparison.
my_number = 35
if my_number < 50:
        print("My number is less than 50")


### This code snippet will generate an error msg:
### The correct statement to compare two values should be: "if my_number == 35"
my_number = 35
if my_number = 35:
        print("My number is less than 50")

### This code snippet will generate an error msg:
### The correct code to assign something to a variable is: "my_number = 35"

my_number == 35
if my_number = 35:
        print("My number is less than 50")
```

Here are variations of the “if”, “if/else” and “if/elif” functions that can be used to test *multiple* conditions.

```
### Using the “if / else” instructions.
my_age = 35
if my_age >= 21:
    print(“I am eligible to vote”)
else:
    print(“I am not eligible to vote.”)


### Using the "if-elif-else" variation.
test_score = 92
if test_score >= 90:
   print("I've made an 'A' on this test.")
elif test_score >= 80:
   print("I've made a 'B' on the test.")
elif test_score >= 70:
   print("I've scored only a 'C' on this test.")
else:
   print("I've failed, and need to put in more study.")
```

An important consideration is that execution of code occurs *when the condition is satisfied.* Because of this, the *order* in which conditions are checked by program flow statements becomes critical in obtaining correct results.

For example; what happens when the conditional test for a "C" grade is *placed above* the "A" conditions in the program lines, as in the following example?

```
### Using the "if-elif-else" statement
test_score = 92
if test_score >= 70:
  print("I've scored only a 'C' on this test.")
elif test_score >= 90:
  print("I've made an 'A' on this test.")
elif test_score >= 80:
  print("I've made a 'B' on the test.")
else:
  print("I've failed, and need to put in more study.")
```

This order of program execution does what might be thought of as a "short-circuit" of the code, returning a result of a "C" grade, even though the student had a test score of 92. Once a condition is satisfied, the rest of the "if /elif /else" block is ignored. Of course, the above order of execution can be coded to work properly, but requires additional elements to ensure it returns correct results. In the following example; note the method of checking the *test_score* variable, testing to see if it falls *within a range,* by using the logical "*and*" operator within the test criteria.

```
### "if-elif-else" variation with logical "AND" conditions
test_score = int(input("What did I score on this exam? "))
if test_score >= 70 and test_score < 80:
  print("I've scored only a 'C' on this test.")
elif test_score >= 80 and test_score < 90:
  print("I've made a 'B' on the test.")
elif test_score >= 90:
  print("I've made an 'A' on this test.")
else:
  print("I've failed, and need to put in more study.")
```

Next, let's look into a simple example that prices a trip to the movie theater. It will use coding that uses both *"and"* & *"or"* comparisons, and asks for the movie-goer's selection of a concession option before providing a tally of the final bill. Shown here are the "f{.2f}" *formatting options* that we used in a previous lesson to limit our result to two decimal places; and the use of the *"augmented assignment operator"*, used to increment a variable by a designated amount.

Sample Code:

```
### Movie Night
print("Welcome to the movie. Ticket prices are as follows:")
print("Youth tickets, age 12 and under: $ 7.00")
print("Adult tickets, 12-55 of age: $ 12.00")
print("Senior tickets, ages 55+:  $ 10.00")
bill = 0
age = int(input("Your age? "))
if age <= 12:
  bill = 7
elif age > 12 and age < 55:
  bill = 12
elif age >= 55:
  bill = 10
print("We have a special on our popcorn and medium drink combo for $12.00")
add_on = input("Would you like popcorn and soft drink?  Select Y / N:  ")
if add_on == "Y" or add_on == "y":          #Yes to concession offer.
  bill +=12
  bill = f"{bill:.2f}"
  print(f"Your bill is $ {bill}")
elif add_on == "N" or add_on == "n":        #No to concession offer.
  bill = f"{bill:.2f}"
  print(f"With no popcorn or drink, your bill is: $ {bill}")
else:                                       #Misc or random keystroke.
  bill = f"{bill:.2f}"
          print(f"OK, your bill is: $ {bill},enjoy the movie.")
```

Notes & Observation:

- The *augmented assignment operator* can be particularly useful within a loop for keeping track of the number of repetitions a section of code has been executed. In the previous example, I've used this method to facilitate an *addition* operation to calculate the total bill, but this same method can also be used to *subtract, multiple* or *divide* by whatever value you set.

- Any selection other than a "Y / N" response by the user, when asked about the popcorn and drink combo offer, will simply pass through the remainder of the program and output the final bill.

- In this example, I've used "or" logic to test for the input of either an uppercase or lowercase response. A useful tool provided by Python for handling string datatypes, is the *lower()* method which, is a built-in method that converts *all* uppercase letters in a string to lowercase, returning it as a new string. Here is an example showing the use of the *lower()* method, just showing the first *three lines* of the "popcorn & drink" section, where the user-responses will be string datatypes and could be entered as either uppercase or lowercase.

Example code:

```
print("We have a special on popcorn and medium drink combo for $12.00")
add_on = input("Would you like popcorn and soft drink? Select Y / N: ").lower()

if add_on == "y":                          #Yes to concession offer.
  conditions
Elif add-on == "n":                        #No to the concession offer.
  conditions
```

As you can see, the words "lower()" is simply added to the end of the statement that requests input for the variable "add_on". Changes are made to eliminate the "or" conditions that test for the uppercase response – since it is no longer necessary. In chapters that follow, we'll look into Python's many built-in functions and methods such as the "lower()" method.

Creating a Flow Chart:

The next program is one that can be used to test whether a "year"; entered as a program input, is a *leap-year*. Of course, to be a leap-year specific criteria must be met, and we'll utilize *nested* "if" statements to verify and then output an appropriate answer. To be a leap year, these specific conditions must be met.

1. The year must be evenly divisible by 4. If not, it is NOT a leap year.
2. If evenly divisible by 4, and NOT by 100 – it is a leap year!
3. If it is evenly divisible by 4, 100 and by 400 – it is a leap year!

Making a flowchart can be a valuable, and often indispensable aid in programming, especially so whenever a result depends upon multiple conditions being satisfied. Here is a simple flowchart, illustrating the listed conditions for determining if a given year is a leap year, and the desired results or outcomes for each tested condition.

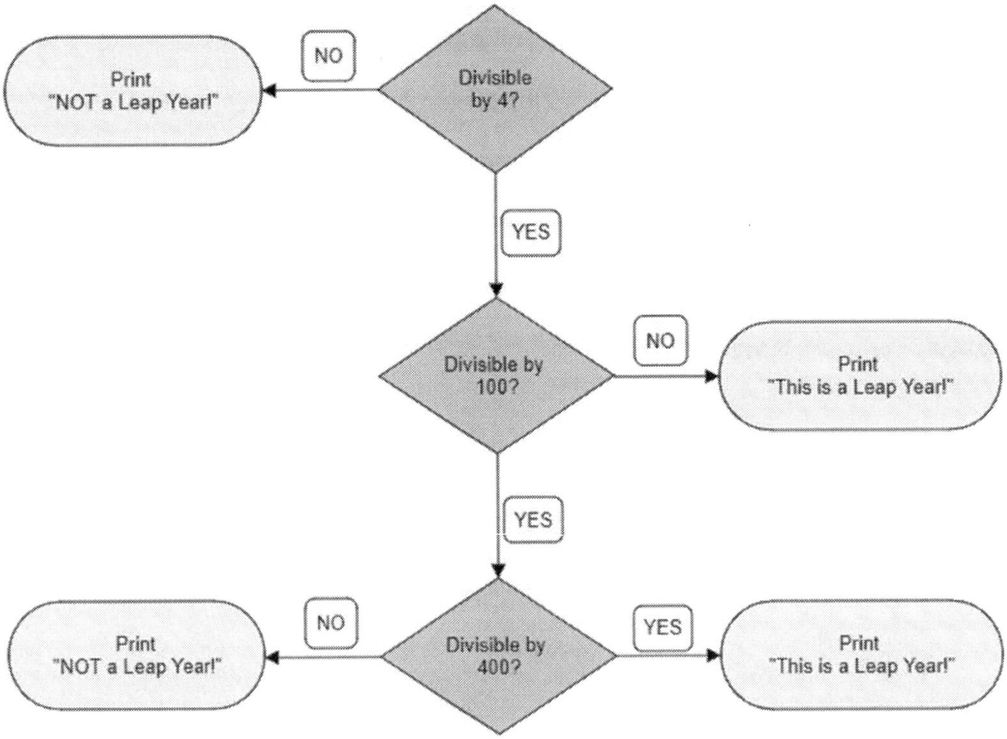

With these conditions in mind, a short program utilizing the "if/else" and "modulo" functions can be used to test these conditions for any year entered as input into the program. In this instance, I've used what is typically referred to as "*nested*" if statements. Remember, when nesting "if" and "if-else" pairs, that each pair will *share the same indentation levels*. Both the IDLE interpreter / editor window, and VS Code editor window will help by automating these indentations, a helpful feature for sure, but it still easy to occasionally miss getting an *elif* or *else* indented at the wrong level. Of course, when you attempt to run the module – the program will let you know if errors exist and corrections are necessary.

Example Code:

```
### Enter any year to see if it is a leap year ###

year = int(input("Enter any year to check if it is a leap year: "))
print("\n")
if year % 4 == 0:
  print(f"Year {year} is evenly divisible by 4. Is it divisible by 100?\n")
  if year % 100 == 0:
    print(f"Year {year} is evenly divisible by 4 and 100; Is it divisible by 400?\n")
    if year % 400 == 0:
      print(f"The year: {year}, is a leap year. It is divisible by 4, 100, and 400!")
    else:
      print(f"The year: {year}, is NOT a leap year.Divisible by 4 & 100, but NOT 400!")
  else:
    print(f"The year: {year}, is a leap year.  Divisible by 4, but not 100!")
else:
  print(f"The year: {year}, is NOT a leap year. It not divisible by 4!")
```

Here is yet another example that uses the “and/or” comparisons in a slightly different way, and in the process makes our coding shorter and more to the point.

```
### Enter any year to see if it is a leap year ###

year = int(input("Enter any year to check if it is a leap year: "))
if (year % 4 == 0 and year % 100 != 0) or (year % 400 == 0):
  print(f"Year {year} is a leap year")
else:
  print(f”The year you’ve selected:  {year} is not a leap year.”)
```

Notes & Observations:

- Note the importance of "indentation" in determining if/else and if/elif pairings.

- Note the use of the *modulo* (%) function, which returns a *remainder*, thus verifying whether a number is *evenly divisible* by the tested conditions.

- There are many ways in which this objective could be programmed.

In this final example of using *nested* if statements; you'll again see that there are multiple methods of accomplishing the same end result. This sample code shows a couple of ways to calculate the final bill on your next pizza order. The criteria are as follows:

Base prices are:

- $15.00 for a small pizza, $20 for a medium pizza, and $25 for a large pizza.

Additional cost for added pepperoni and added cheese:

- $2.00 for a small, and $3.00 for the medium or large.
- Upcharge for added cheese is $1.00 for any size of pizza.
- Include an 8.5% tax for the final customer bill.

Example 1 Code:

```
### Pizza Order
size = input("What size of pizza would you like: S, M, or L: ")
add_pepperoni = input("Would you like to add pepperoni: Y or N? ")
add_cheese = input("Do you want extra cheese:  Y or N? ")
bill = 0
if size == "S" or size == "s":
    if add_pepperoni == "Y" or add_pepperoni == "y":
        if add_cheese == "Y" or add_cheese == "y":
            bill = 15 + 2 + 1
        else:
            bill = 15 + 2
    elif add_cheese == "Y" or add_cheese == "y":
            bill = 15 + 1
    else:
            bill = 15
```

```
if size == "M" or size == "m":
  if add_pepperoni == "Y" or add_pepperoni == "y":
    if add_cheese == "Y" or add_cheese == "y":
      bill = 20 + 3 + 1
    else:
      bill = 20 + 3
  elif add_cheese == "Y" or add_cheese == "y":
      bill = 20 + 1
  else:
      bill = 20
if size == "L" or size == "l":
  if add_pepperoni == "Y" or add_pepperoni == "y":
    if add_cheese == "Y" or add_cheese == "y":
      bill = 25 + 3 + 1
    else:
      bill = 25 + 3
  elif add_cheese == "Y" or add_cheese == "y":
      bill = 25 + 1
  else:
      bill = 25
final_bill = round((bill * 1.085), 2)
print("Thank you for your order:")
print(f"Your final bill is: ${final_bill}.")
```

This next example is quite a bit shorter. It uses the *lower()* method, and once again shows the use of the "*augmented assignment operator*". It gives you the ability to *increase or decrease* the value within a variable, by using a math operator in combination with an equal sign. In this scenario, it enables us to keep a sort of running-tally on the pizza bill, as we simply test through all the conditions (options) for our pizza order. As you can see, even with the nested "if" statements, it is only 23 lines of code including the header, and more straightforward to read.

Example 2 Code:

```
### Pizza Order
size = input("What size of pizza would you like: S, M, or L: ").lower()
add_pepperoni = input("Would you like pepperoni: Y or N? ").lower()
add_cheese = input("Do you want extra cheese:  Y or N? ").lower()
bill = 0
if size == "s":
  bill += 15
elif size == "m":
  bill += 20
else:
  bill += 25
if add_pepperoni == "y":
  if size == "s":
    bill += 2
  else:
    bill += 3
if add_cheese == "y":
  bill += 1
final_bill = round((bill * 1.085),2)
print("Thank you for your order:")
print(f"Your final bill is: ${final_bill}.")
```

Notes & Observations:

- Just for some "hands-on" practice, draw a simple flow chart based on the initial conditions or criterial shown.

Lesson 9: Using "For" and "While" Loops

In Python, *loops* unlock the power of repetition and automation, and form one of the core building blocks of efficient programming. Whether you're cycling through a range of numbers, processing a list of customer orders, or performing complex simulations, loops make it possible while using just a few lines of code. This chapter will focus and walk you through some basic examples of using methods of iteration: the *for* and *while* loop, and in the process will make your code shorter, smarter, and easier to maintain.

Coding "for" and "while" loops into a program, gives us a method of repeating sets of instructions to achieve a desired outcome. Each repetition of a process is referred to as an *iteration*. In programming, *iteration* is commonly used to:

- Process data that is contained within a sequence, such as a list, tuple or array.
- Perform repeated calculations or operations.
- Automate repetitive tasks until a condition is met.

For example, in Python:

- A *"for loop"* iterates over a list or range, executing the block of code for *each item in the sequence.*
- A *"while loop"* iterates as long as a *specified condition* is met or *true.*

As you can see in examples that follow, iteration methods facilitate the completion of specific programming objectives – even very simple ones, and are fundamental to problem-solving in programming. Iteration enables developers to efficiently handle repetitive tasks without the use of redundant code, making code blocks cleaner and easier to understand.

The For Loop:

Use the "*for loop*" to iterate over a sequence datatype, such as a list, tuple, or string:

- The ***for*** keyword *initiates the loop,* indicating your desire to perform an action for each item in the sequence.
- The ***in*** keyword *specifies the sequence.*

Here are some basic examples of "*for*" loops, and how they work within your code. Take some time coding these, and then maybe experiment with variations such as using tuples or dictionary data sequences.

Sample code 1:

```
# For Loop Iteration using the "for" and "in" keywords
# Using a mix of datatypes within the list sequence
fruit_list = ["banana", "apple", 12345, "orange", "pear", 46.821, "Plum"]
for fruit in fruit_list:
    print(fruit)
    print(type(fruit))          # Prints each type of objects in list.
print("\n All the items listed in 'fruit_list' have now been printed!")
```

Sample code 2:

```
# Iteration using a For Loop to total a group of test scores.
test_scores = [ 89,100,94,96,68,82,97,100,84,92,62,69,76,70,82]
print(test_scores)
scr_total = 0
for i in test_scores:
    scr_total += i
    print(f"Running Total of all test scores: {scr_total}")
print(f"\nFinal Total of all test scores is:  {scr_total}")
```

Sample code 3:

```
# Using the "for" and "in" keywords with a range of integer values.
# Using a nested “if/else” and the “modulo” function.
num = 0
for num in range(1, 26):
  if num % 3 == 0 and num % 2 == 0:
    print("Python")
  else:
    print(num)
```

Sample code 4:

```
# Nested For Loops to build a Multiplication table
count = int(input("Build a ‘Multiplication Table’ for 'How many Numbers'??  "))
for i in range(1, count+1):
   for n in range(1, count+1):
     print(f"{i} x {n} = {i * n}")
```

Sample code 5:

```
# Iteration over a string variable, prints each character in the string.
for char in "Hello World":
  print(char)
```

Sample code 6:

```
# Iteration over dictionary that will print key:value pairs.
person = {"name": "Andy", "age": 60, "city": "Denver"}
for key, value in person.items():
  print(key, ":", value)
```

The While Loop:

Next shown, is an example of looping that uses the *while* keyword. Remember that the "while" keyword will call for the repetition of the indexed instructions below it, as long as the specific conditions continue to be met or "true". Code execution leaves the iterated loop when conditions are no longer true, and continues executing the remaining program. Here are two simple examples of using a *while loop*:

Sample 1 "While" loop:

```
# Using While Loop Iterations

num_select = int(input("How many iterations would you like to display? "))
loop_count = 0
while loop_count < num_select:
    loop_count +=1
    print(f"This is the {loop_count} iteration of this 'While' loop.")
num_select = 0
print(f"The loop_count is now {loop_count}, Exit the Loop.")
print(f"Looping is complete, iteration number reset to {num_select}.")
```

Sample 2 "While" Loop:

```
# Using While Loop Iteration and an embedded "nested" "if" condition.
num_select = int(input("How many iterations would you like to display? "))
loop_count = 0
while loop_count < num_select:
    loop_count +=1
    print(f"This is the {loop_count} iteration of this 'While' loop.")
    if loop_count % 2 == 0:
      print(f"Loop Count {loop_count} is a 'EVEN' number.")
num_select = 0
print(f"The loop_count is now {loop_count}, Exit the Loop.")
print(f"Looping is complete, iteration number has reset to {num_select}.")
```

Notes & Observations:

- The *while* section of code is initiated by specific criteria or conditions being met; in these examples, *loop_count* being less than the value we've entered into *num_select.*

- It will continue repeating, *not exiting the while loop* as long as these conditions continue to be met.

- Observe in that "*num_select*" isn't reset to zero (0) until all iterations have completed, and execution has exited the while loop.

- Observe that other conditional statements and loops can be "nested" within a main section "while" loop.

Lesson 10: Object Oriented Programming

Object Oriented Programming, typically referenced as OOP, is a paradigm that focuses upon writing and building code around common functional groups. These groupings then become more "portable", in their ability to be used within your programs. An important concept within Python's OOP environment, starts with the development of these reuseable, modular groups of code. Many of the most popular and widely used programming languages, including Java, JavaScript, C++, C#, Swift, PHP, and a host of others, follow the OOP paradigm. In keeping with OOP principles; Python uses common contructs referred to as *classes*, *modules, methods, functions, and objects* as the building blocks upon which a Python program is built. To better understand how Python integrates OOP, we'll take a more in-depth look into *modules* and *functions*.

Modules:

A module, as you've already noticed when using the *math module*, is a repository or library for numerous *functions*, and can also be used to hold methods, lists, or variables. After "importing" a module into your code structure, any methods, functions, or other data it contains, can be *called* and used throughout a program. This is done by first designating the *module* and *function,* using "dot" notation between *module* and *function;* and finally, any *parameters*, *arguments, or variables you want the function to act upon,* as shown in the following examples:

Examples of using *math module* functions

Import math

- result1 = math.sqrt(25)   # Returns 5.0 into result1.
- my_angle = math.degrees(math.pi) # Converts PI from radians to degrees.
- sqr_val = math.sqrt(my_number)   # Place sq-root of *my_number* into *sqr_val*.

Any program you create, having a ".py" extension, is essentially a "module". So; following OOP principles, we can create a "module" that serves as a container for all the variables, functions, classes, methods, or sequence lists that we develop. Creating this new module is basically as straightforward as creating a new python program. The differences reside in the fact that this module will contain functions and code that; for the most part, are not standalone code. Our created module will need to be *referenced* by a *user program*, and its *functions and methods* will need to be *called* into action by that program. Like any other module, once imported, all of its functions can be used by your programs to accomplish specific programming objectives. Next, let's look more deeply into functions, with some examples on how we can create both modules and functions, and use these important elements in our programming.

Functions:

Functions are comprised of code that performs a specific task, but are *not directly attached* or associated with any specific *class-defined object*. By now, you've become familiar and have practiced using the *print(), type(), len(), int(), str(), float(), max(), min(), range()*, and *input()* functions. These functions can be used, at any point within a program, and so are often referred to as *built-in functions*. These exist within the Python instructional set and can be called directly *at any point* in the program. As shown in previous examples and sample code snippets, the syntax format for calling a function into action is simply to enter the function name, and include any arguments within the parenthesis. The function acts upon the argument, and returns a value.

Here are some typical examples – shown and used earlier.

input function: Prints output to the string argument, and waits for a user response. Places the user-response into a variable called *my_number*.

- my_number = input("Enter any number: ")

function within a function: First executes the *input* function, obtaining a string value, then converts the string into an integer value, placing it into the *"my_number"* variable.

- my_number = int(input("Enter any number: "))

We can also define and create our own unique functions; blocks of code that may be used repeatedly within a program; or, if placed within a module, can be imported and used by any program we create. This saves time and effort by alleviating repetitive coding for every instance where a specific task is necessary. Here's an example of creating a *user-defined* function, and an example of how that function might be used in a short example program.

The first step is to create the function itself. We accomplish this by *defining* the function using the "def" keyword. We then name the function, and add any parameters that we may need. These parameters, are the containers or *placeholders* that will receive the values *(arguments)* passed into the function from your program. The definition (DEF) line will always end with a colon (:). When the Python interpreter sees the colon, it automatically indexes the next line, much like the "if" statements shown in previous examples. These indexed lines of code are what the function executes when called by your main program. Here is an example of creating and using a simple function that prints "Hello World" whenever specific conditions are met, and loops through the program for the number of times you have chosen.

```
# Hello World Counter #

def hello(num):                        # Define the function "hello".
  if num % 3 == 0 and num % 5 == 0:    # If <num> is evenly divisible by 3 & 5.
    print("Hello World!")              # Print "Hello World"
  else:
    print(num)                         # Otherwise, just print the number.

# User program that calls the function
a = 0
count = int(input("How many numbers? "))     # Select how many numbers to test.
for a in range(1, count+1):                  # Call the "hello" function until a = count
  hello(a)

# Note: in the "for" loop, "a" is passed into "num" whenever the "hello" function is called. It is
then called until count+1 is reached.
```

In the next example, we'll obtain a name from user response within the main program, and then pass this variable *into* the function call parameter. In this example; as in the previous example, the function "hello" also handles the actual print execution. Try out this first code example, making sure you understand the *program flow* and what is happening during each step. As shown below, the second example has a problem and generates an error.

Examples of *user-program, and user-defined function*:

Example 1:

```
# Created "hello" function #
def hello(arg1):            # Define a function named "hello"
   print("Hello, ", arg1)   # Note: argument separated by a comma
# Main user program #
name = input("Greetings, what is your name? ")  # Obtains the user <name>
hello(name)                                     # Calls the function "hello"
#Output: Hello, <name>                          # Prints <name> from user.
```

What happens if the function "def" is placed *after* the function call, as in this example?

Example 2:

```
# Main user program #
name = input("Greetings, what is your name? ")  # Obtains user <name>
hello(name)                                     # Calls the function "hello"


# Created "hello" function #
def hello(arg1):                                # Define the function: "hello".
  print("Hello, ", arg1)

#Output Error Message:
NameError: name 'hello' is not defined'.
```

As you can see from this, our function has to be defined *before* being called into action. Our program executes in a top/down fashion – line-by-line. It's interesting to note, that this becomes less of a potential problem when our function; or multiple functions for that matter, are *put into a module* and then called when needed. When a "module" is first imported into a user-program; all of the functions it contains – *defined at the module level*, are parsed and stored as *callable objects*, but are not executed until explicitly called. To show a simple example of this, here are two created functions for different greetings, both placed within a single module I've named the "greetings_module".

Create a Module:

Example of a User-created Module: the "greetings" module:

```
greetings.py
def hello (arg1):
   print ("Hello, ", arg1)

def goodbye (arg1):
   print ("Goodbye,", arg1)
```

As you can see, this module holds the *two functions*, both of which use the same argument name (arg1). This is okay, because "*arg1*" is only a container to hold whatever value we pass into it, and will be referenced when its *function* is called by a user-program. With the functions now created; we next need to code a *user program* to access the module, along with its associated functions. Here is an example program that calls and uses this module and its functions. This example passes a variable *into* the function parameter, where the respective functions print different responses.

```
# User program "hello-goodbye.py"

   import greetings

   # Obtain the user responses.
   name = input("What is your name? ")
   leaving = input("Are you leaving for the day?  Y or N: ").upper()

   # Call the applicable function that is within the module "greetings".
   if leaving == "Y":
      greetings.goodbye(<name>)
   else:
      greetings.hello(<name>)
```

Obtaining a "Return" value:

A different scenario, although very typical, is for the user-defined function to pass a value *back into the user-program.* This is accomplished by using the "*return*" keyword, as shown in the following example:

```
# User-defined functions, common arguments, and multiple return values #

    def calc_product(arg1, arg2):
        return arg1 * arg2

    def calc_exp(arg1, arg2):
        return pow(arg1, arg2)

    # User program:
    x = float(input("Select a number for variable 'x':  "))
    y = float(input("Select a number for variable 'y': "))

    result1 = calc_product(x,y)
    result2 = calc_exp(x,y)

    print(f"'x' times 'y' is equal to: {result1:.2f}")

    print(f"'x' raised to the power of 'y' equals: {result2:.2f}")
```

As you can see from running this program; once the function is called, it passes the user-input for "x" and "y" into the respective function. The function performs a calculation, and *returns* the value back to the user-program variables – "*result1*" and "*result2*". Play with this code a bit, making sure you fully understand the "*back and forth*" and "*line-by-line*" nature of the program execution.

Here is another example of a user-created module I've named "*my_calc.py*". It contains a simple user-defined function called "*do_the_math*". My user program, named "Perform_math.py", functions as a basic calculator program, but needs the "my_calc.py" module to do the work. Take some time to code this, dissect and re-create it with some of your own changes, maybe even coding some additional math functions.

Note that in the function definition, I've used as parameters the letters (x, y, z), but of course any names you choose will work as long as those same arguments are used in the *code sections of the function.* We could just as easily code the line: *return var1 + var2,* the names really don't matter, as long as they are defined and used consistently throughout your function code.

Summary for the Calculator program:

- A user-response is obtained and placed into the string variable "*op*" as the user decides *what math operation* to perform.

- Numeric values are entered and placed into "*num1*" and "*num2*". Note that additional variables could be obtained which might be used on other types of math functions. All variables need place-holders (parameters) within the function definition.

- When the function "*do_the_math*" is actually called, the "*op*" variable (argument) is passed to the function into the position "z" parameter. Values for parameters "x" and "y", are also obtained from user-input, and passed into the function as well. This is based on the "order" in which the argument values are listed in the function call.

- At this point, the "if / elif / else" conditions take over, providing flow control to direct execution to the portion of code that handles the desired math operation.

- Returns a value back to the main user program function call, and putting that value into a floating-point variable called "result".

Created *module*: *"my_calc.py"*, containing a single *function* named: *"do_the_math"*

my_calc.py

```
def do_the_math(x, y, z):            # Define the function
  if z == "A":
    return x + y
  elif z == "S":
    return x - y
  elif z == "M":
    return x*y
  elif z == "D":
    if y!= 0:
      return x / y
    else:
      print("Sorry - you can't divide by zero. Give it another go!")
      return 0000
  elif z == "E":
    return pow(x, y)
```

 # User program #

```
import my_calc

op = input("Add, Subtract, Multiply, Divide, Exponent? KEY the first letter:").upper()
num1 = float(input("Select a value for 'x'; "))
num2 = float(input("Select a value for 'y': "))
```

 # Calls the function, passes variables to the function, and receives return value

```
result = my_calc.do_the_math(num1, num2, op)
```

 # Format result and print #

```
print(f"Answer from calculation is: {result:.2f}")   # Formats floating point result.
```

Notes and Observations:

- Multiple functions, defined at a module level, can be called by any user program that has imported that module.

- The "import *module*" code is typically placed at the beginning of your user program code.

- When *calling* a function that resides within a module, the module name must be referenced first, followed by the function name. A period is used as the separator between module and function, as shown again in these examples.

```
# Calls "goodbye" from the "greetings" module.
greetings.goodbye(<name>)

# Calls "do_the_math" from the "my_calc" module.
result = my_calc.do_the_math(num1, num2, op)
```

Methods:

A *method* is similar to a function; in that it performs specific tasks, but yet not quite the same either. *Methods are associated or linked to a class and its objects.* A class is often referred to as a "blueprint" for creating objects. Class defines the data-structure *attributes* (variables), and the *functions* that determine the behavior of an object. *Functions defined within a "class" structure are referred to as "methods".*

You invoke or *call* a method to act *upon* an object, such as a string variable, a list, a tuple, or other datatype. An example of this, shown earlier, was the usage of *lower()* on the string we acquired from an input statement. The *lower()* method is *associated and used* with the string (str) *class of objects*. Here are a few other *methods* associated with - and commonly used, on the string class of objects: *lower(), upper(), strip(), title(), swapcase(),* and *capitalize().*

```
op = input("Add, Subtract, Multiply, Divide, or Exponent?").upper()

my_name = input("What is your name? ").strip(),.title()
```

Invoking the *strip()* method will *strip away any extra spaces* located *before* or *after* the name. These extra spaces may have been keyed - perhaps accidentally, by the user into the input string. If so, the *strip()* method will take care of this potential problem.

The *title()* method will *capitalize the first letters* on the first and last name. Here is a short program where you can test several of these methods to view how they work on a user-input string.

```
## Using some built-in String Methods ##

name=input("Enter your name with any case or extra spacing you choose: ")

method_test=input("Enter the 'method' you want to test? 'strip', 'swapcase', 'title', or 'capitalize';
").lower()


if method_test == "strip":
  print(name)
  striped_name=(name).strip()
  print(striped_name)
  print(len(striped_name))


elif method_test == "swapcase":
  print(method_test)
  print(name)
  changed_case_name=(name).swapcase()
  print(changed_case_name)
```

```
elif method_test == "title":
  print(method_test)
  print(name)
  first_last=(name).title()
  print(first_last)


elif method_test == "capitalize":
  print(method_test)
  print(name)
  print(len(name))
  all_cap_name=(name).capitalize()
  print(all_cap_name)
  print(len(all_cap_name))
```

Here is an example that illustrates the use of *multiple methods* being integrated into a single line of code.

```
## Using multiple methods in a single line of code ##

name=input("What is your name??, please enter it here: ").strip().title()
print(name)
print(len(name))
```

Finally, I'd like to show the "append" method, which is used to add new data to a list, or to sort values and repopulate another list. Enter this short coding example that examines the usage of the append() method to add values to a list.

Using the "append()" Method:

```
# Using the append() #

fruit_list = ["apple", "pear", "peach", "plum", "apricot"]
add_on = input("What fruit would you like to add to your list? ")
fruit_list.append(add_on)
print(fruit_list)
```

Notes: While *Functions* and *Methods* are similar in some respects, they are different in the syntax used in how they are called into use.

Function only use:	input("What is your name? ") # *function(<string>)*
Function Call from import module:	math.sqrt(my_number) # *module.function(arg)*
Function & Methods Combined:	my_name = input("Enter your name? ").strip(),.title()

Lesson 11: More on Modules

It should be quite evident by now, that modules are pre-built, ready-to-use blocks of code, and key components of the OOP style of programming. Back in Lesson 7, I introduced just a few of the functions included within the ***math*** module. In those chapters, we looked into using the *rounding* and *absolute number functions*, and one that returns the *square-root* or *log of a number*. All of these, and more, are contained within the math module. Accessing the Python math module saves us the trouble of having to perform repetitive coding, makes coding more efficient, and gives us an easier method of dealing with complex and repetitive operations. Because of their importance, I'd like to introduce some other modules that you may find useful; and more importantly, get more accustomed to integrating into your coding.

In this lesson, we'll begin with the ***random*** module, a module that contains different functions for *generating random numbers*. While this may not sound very exciting, it is a critical component for modeling unpredictability and impartiality in statistical sampling, encryption, and simulating other real-world scenarios. Python provides some methods to make random values fairly straightforward to integrate into our coding. Just like when we used the math module, we'll first need to *call-up* the *random module* by coding the "*import random*" statement early in our code.

In the following examples, we'll briefly look into using three different random module functions: the *randint* function, the *random* function, and finally the *uniform* function. All of these will return random values, as well as different types of numeric values. For example; when we code the function, *random.randint(0, 5)* into our program and execute, it will return an integer value in that range of 0, 1, 2, 3, 4, or 5 each time it is executed. Note the *inclusivity* of the end-point numbers listed within the parenthesis, and that it returns an integer rather than a floating-point number. We'll use this functionality to build a program that mimics a coin flip. We'll also use many of the concepts we've discussed, including a looping method shown in a previous chapter: the "*while loop*". This will repeat sections of code until a specific condition is satisfied. Just like when using nested "if-elif-else" statements, remember that care must be taken with indentations, as this determines the pairing of conditions within specific sections of code. Note the simple method of *incrementing* or *decrementing* a value needed to continue in the "while-loop" for a specified number of times. In this example program, we'll perform datatype conversions, and use a math operation in calculating percentages that "heads" or "tails" are tallied. You may have other ideas or methods you want to try, and I encourage you to do so. The important idea in programming is to make the code your own, and experimenting with different ideas in arriving at an objective or desired result.

Sample Code: Using the *randint(a, b)* function.

```
# Heads or Tails #
import random                              # Invokes the random module for usage in your code.
num_toss = 0                               # Initialize variables to zero
heads = 0
tails = 0
h_perc = 0
t_perc = 0

num_toss = int(input("How many times shall we toss the coin? "))
sel_num = num_toss


while num_toss > 0:
  num_toss -= 1                            # decrements num_toss within our "while loop".
  coin_toss = random.randint(0, 1)         # Select random integer of (0) or (1).
  if coin_toss == 1:
    print("The coin is Heads!")
    heads += 1                             # Running total of "Heads".
  else:
    print("The coin is Tails!")
    tails += 1                             # Running total of "Tails".
```

```
else:                                   # exits the "while loop" if num_toss is <= to 0
  print(f"This completes {sel_num} coin flips!")
  h_perc = (100 *(float(heads / sel_num)))
  h_perc = round(h_perc, 2)
  t_perc = (100 *(float(tails / sel_num)))
  t_perc = round(t_perc, 2)
  print(f"Heads won {h_perc} percent of the time.")
  print(f"Tails won {t_perc} percent of the time.")
```

Here is a slightly different and easier way of coding the coin toss application by using another of the random module tools; the "choice" function. It also shows how we can use a "*for*" loop for our selected number or "*range*" of coin tosses.

Sample Code: Using the *choice(a, b)* function

```
import random

# Get the number of tosses from user
tosses = int(input("Select the number of coin tosses: "))
# Set initial count values
heads = 0
tails = 0
# Simulate the coin tosses
for _ in range(tosses):
  toss = random.choice(["heads", "tails"])
  if toss == "heads":
    heads += 1
  else:
    tails += 1
# Calculate the percentages
h_perc = (heads / tosses) * 100
t_perc = (tails / tosses) * 100

# Display percentages with formatting
print(f"\nFor {tosses} number of coin tosses, there were {heads} heads, and {tails} tails!")
print(f"The percentage of heads was: {h_perc:.2f}%")
print(f"The percentage of tails was:  {t_perc:.2f}%")
```

Here are a few additional functions contained within the ***random*** module. The function used in the following example, "*random()*", returns a *float number* between 0 and 1, non-inclusive of 1. Therefore, the value returned (n) is ($0.0 <= n < 1.0$). This function might be used together with another function contained in the "random" module, the "*randint()*" function. Using these together allows you to generate larger random floating-point numbers, as determined by the values entered as arguments within the parenthesis.

Sample Code: Using the *random()* and *randint(a, b)* functions.
Turning integer values into random floating-point numbers.

```
import random
num_select = int(input("How many random numbers would you like to display? "))
loop_count = 0

while loop_count < num_select:
   random_int = random.randint(1, 10)                  #Generate random integer of 1 through 10
   random_float = random.random()                      #Generate random float: (0.0 <= n < 1.0)

# Creates a larger floating point number #
   generated_value= (random_float * random_int)
   generated_value = round(generated_value,3)
   print(f"The random float value is now: {generated_value}.")
   loop_count +=1
else:
   print(f"Your number generator has displayed {loop_count} random numbers.")
   num_select = 0
```

You may want to experiment with different aspects of this code, such as the range of values, rounding, or how the output is displayed. As you can see in this example, the output of "generated_value" will never be equal to 10 (or whatever value you set for the high-end of the range), and always contains a fractional *(decimal)* value.

Next, let's take a brief look into the use of the *uniform(a, b)* function. The *uniform* function returns *float numbers* that are within the values you set within the instruction, *inclusive of the lower value* and *exclusive of the upper end-point value.*

- Therefore; for program line: n = random.uniform(1, 10)
- The output "*n*" would be a *random floating point value*: (a <= *n* < b).

Sample Code: Using the *uniform(a, b)* function.

```
### Using the Random Module, uniform function

import random

num_select = int(input("How many random numbers would you like to display? "))
loop_count = 0

while loop_count < num_select:
  random_float = random.uniform(1, 10)
  random_float = round(random_float, 2)
  print(f"The generated random floating point number is: {random_float}")
  loop_count +=1
else:
  print(f"Your number generator has displayed {loop_count} random numbers.")
  num_select = 0
```

We've explored just a few of the functions contained within the *math* and *random* modules, but there are many others available. For example; there are code applications for statistics, and for the tools you might need when working with complex numbers.

Finally, for these last examples, I'd like to briefly look into the ***heapq*** module. It contains functions that can be used in manipulating *collections of data*; such as lists or tuples, and is interesting enough that it merits spending some time exploring its usage. It is typically used to pull minimum or maximum values from an array or list, and useful for *sorting* data within a list.

In this next example I'll use the "*heapq*" module to pull values from a list and place then into a different, newly created list.

First, a look at two different functions belonging to the heapq module: the *nlargest()* and the *nsmallest()* functions. Both are useful for returning values from a list.

```
## Using the nlargest() and the nsmallest() functions ##
import heapq
my_list = [10, 5, 8, 3, 48, 20, 1, 15]

top_three = heapq.nlargest(3, my_list)           # Get the three largest elements
bottom_three = heapq. nsmallest(3, my_list)      # Get the three smallest elements
print(top_three)
print(bottom_three)
```

Once again, note the syntax shown in these examples. As a function defined within a module, the *module name* must precede the *function name*, which precedes any *arguments*, using the "dot" notation for module and function separation.

In the following example, the *heapq* module is used again, this time with some different functions, the *heapify()* and the *heappop()*. The first to *take the smallest value from our list and position it into index [0],* and the second function to *place the [0] position integers into a variable that will be added (appended) into another list in ascending order.*

```
## Using heapify() and heappop() functions ##
import heapq
new_list = []                                    # Create a new list, currently empty.
my_list = [27, 2, 7, 63, 10, 17]

# Print the original, unsorted list.
print("The original unsorted LIST called 'my_list' is:  ", my_list)

# Set-up a loop for the number of values in "my_list".
loops = 0
while loops < 6:
  heapq.heapify(my_list)                   # Bring the smallest element to [0] index position
  next_num = heapq.heappop(my_list)  # Put the [0] value into next_num variable
  print(f"The number removed from 'my_list' is: {next_num}")
  print("The remaining values within 'my_list' are:  ", my_list)
  new_list.append(next_num)                      # Put the value into my new_list
  loops += 1                                     # add "1" to the loops count
else:
  print(f"At completion, the new list, in ascending order is: {new_list}")
```

Note the use of the "f-string" method in this last print function line. This could also be coded as it was in line 6 to not include the "f" and simply use: **new_list,** outside of the exclamation symbols.

One of the strengths of Python is the ability to handle and manipulate large amounts of data. Here, I'm only using a six-element list – but it could also be a database containing thousands of values. What if we wanted results to be a list of descending ordered values? How could this be done? What happens if you place a "hash-tag" (#) on the line of code where the *heapify(my_list)* isn't executed? Try this and examine your output to see some different results. As you will see, the "*heappop*" function still pulls the [0] index value from the original list, but it is no longer the smallest value, it is simply the value in the [0] index position. The "*heapify*" function is necessary to push the smallest value of the list into the [0] index position.

In Summary:

To utilize various modules, functions, and methods, you need to:

1. Import the module(s): simply place the statement near the beginning of your code. For example: *import random* or *import math.*
2. Use the desired function within your code. For example:
    - random.*uniform*(1, 10), *random* is the module, *uniform* the function, the values of 1 through 10 are the function arguments.
    - random.*randint*(0, 1), again *random* is the module, *randint* the function using the arguments of 0 and 1.
    - heapq.*heapify*(my_list) where *heapq* designates the module, *heapify* the function, and the list named "my_list" is the *argument* value.
3. Place the *output* of a function or method into a variable as needed for usage within the user program.
    - sq_root_value = math.sqrt(int(my_number))
    - random_float = random.uniform(1, 10)
    - coin_toss = random.randint(0, 1)
    - new_list.append(next_num)

Lesson 12: Putting it all Together:

Python is "Object Oriented Programming" (OOP). Therefore, it is a library comprised of classes and modules, each having key component methods, functions, constants and keywords. Some of these classes and modules are referred to simply as *built-ins*. These *built-in classes* provide functions and methods that are immediately accessible, without requiring you to define or pull them from a module.

An example of a *built-in class* is the string (str) class.

- A string is an *immutable* sequence of characters, such as "hello world", 'my_name', "1492", and such.

- The string itself is referred to as the *object*, in terms of OOP. All of the following are valid instances of string *objects*, including the empty string.

  my_name = "John Smith"
  my_age = "35"
  empty_val = ""

- The string *class* provides *functions* and *methods* to manipulate and work with strings.

  Built-in Functions for string objects: len(), str(), input(), and print() are examples we've used throughout previous lessons.

  Built-in Methods for string objects: upper(), lower(), strip(), title(), capitalize(), replace(*old, new*), split(*separator*), join(*iterable*), find(*substring*), startswith(*prefix*), and count(*substring*).

- Additional built-in classes for Python you may want to explore:

    Integer (int)
    Floating-point (float)
    Boolean (bool)
    List (list)
    Tuple (tuple)
    Dictionary (dict)
    Set (set)
    Frozen Set (frozenset)
    Bytes (bytes)
    Byte Array (bytearray)
    Complex Number (complex)

Here is an additional *built-in class*, the List (list) class, that you've used numerous times in the previous lesson examples, without having to import the class or its modules.

List class summary:

- A list is a mutable, ordered collection of items. These items are separated by comma, contained by square-brackets, and can be a mix of datatypes within the list.

```
my_list = [2, 4, "Hello World", 3.14159, "123456"]
```

- An important characteristic of a "list" is that it is dynamic. Items in a list can be removed or added.

- Built-in Methods used for working with list objects include:

  append(): Adds an item to a list

  extend(): Adds all items from one list to another list.

  insert(i, x): Inserts item (x) into index position (i)

  remove (x): Removes the first occurrence of "x" in a list.

  pop(i): Removes and returns the item at index position (i).

  clear (): Removes all items in a list.

  index(x): Returns the index position of the first occurrence of "x".

  count(x): Returns the number of occurrences of "x".

  sort(x): Sorts the list in place in ascending order.

  reverse(): Reverses the order of the list.

- These built-in methods are utilized in your code by simply entering the *list-name*, followed by the *method* you desire. This method "takes action" upon the named list. Here again is a brief example:

```
my_list = [2, 6, 1, 4, 10]
my_list.sort()     # my_list is sorted to [1, 2, 4, 6, 10]
my_list.pop(4)  # my_list becomes [1, 2, 4, 6]
```

Class or Module?

Next, we'll consider some of Python's "non-built-in" classes and modules – those in which you *must* first import the module in order to utilize its functions and methods. These are included within *Python's Standard Library*. You can also create user-defined classes, just like you earlier defined your own custom modules and functions. These, along with many other third-party classes, can be imported and used in your programming projects.

Here are several Standard Library modules, available once you import the respective module, and each having accessible functions and methods. These are not a comprehensive list, and can be explored further by visiting Python's Help section and the Standard Reference Library.

- datetime module
- collections module
- threading module
- queue module
- os module:
- pathlib module
- re module
- io module
- argparse module
- fractions module

Sometimes It's just a Module:

Modules can be thought of as "toolkits" that contain useful functions, methods and constants. It's helpful to remember that modules differ from classes. Classes are used to *define the properties or characteristics of an object you want to create, or perhaps is already created.* Note however; that some types of modules are used to define and utilize classes. An example of this type of *class-defining* module, would be the "pathlib" module, shown in the above list. It provides ways of interacting with files and directories, and provides the means for creating and editing "path" objects, as shown:

```
from pathlib import Path                    # pathlib is a module, "Path" is the class
path = Path("your_folder/your_file.txt")    # Creates a path object
```

Other modules, the types discussed in this beginner-level book, are entirely present to provide procedural functionality. Examples of these types of modules would include the "*random*", the "*heapq*", and the "*math*" modules. As shown in earlier lessons, these modules can be imported, and their respective functions used in our coding. Among the math modules "toolkit", are functions that handle trigonometric, logarithmic and exponential equations; as well as angular conversions. Similar to this, each module contains its own unique set of methods and functions that will work with specific types of data.

In the last pages of this step-by-step guide, I've tried to revisit the concepts we've covered; and to leave you with some idea of the greater capabilities for using Python. Even though most of the program examples shown throughout this book have been somewhat simple; the concepts they show are the principle building blocks for developing a solid foundation in programming. In keeping with this idea of using the concepts learned thus far, I've included some final examples which I'll summarize below. These examples utilize the OOP construct of defining a *class,* and hopefully will bring some clarity about *classes* and why implementing them can be an advantage. It also, in the final example, introduces a few new keywords that are interesting, and useful. At the end of this section, I'll suggest some modifications and ideas that you may like to integrate into this program, and also how to compile it into an executable program.

Defining and Using a Class:

Here's a Python application that uses a defined class to build objects, manage student information, and calculate a current average of daily grades. Again, my aim is to show examples of how *classes* are used in programming applications. I'll show four different examples or variations of a program; but in general, all four use a defined class, and will include methods that accomplish the following.

Define a Student class with:

- Using the Constructor (__init__) that takes name and student_id
- A list to store grades
- Method to add grades and append them to a list
- Method to calculate a grade average
- Method to display information (display_info)
- A main() function, or fields that allows for student information to be added or edited.
- Allows adding multiple grades
- Display final results

Example 1:

In this example of defining and using a "class", note that the "*user program*" is simply a part of the *single program* that utilizes the "Student" class structure. It isn't a separate thing—it's just the code you use to create and edit each "Student object". Each student *is the object*, so new students can be added – using the same framework, and additional grades can be added to any existing student. When these changes occur, the program would need to be executed once again for the changes to take effect, and new output displayed.

The class definition (class Student: ...) is the framework that defines each object you'll create, whether a single object (IE: "Alice"), or many objects (IE: "Mary", "Bob" and "Gary"). As you can see, creating a class can be useful whenever objects need to be defined in terms of *related data* (IE: name, student ID), and *behaviors* (IE: calculate a grade average, list all grades for the student, show student's info).

```
# Here's the defined Student class with the user-program portion included into a single file:

class Student:

 def __init__(self, name, student_id):
    self.name = name                          # Student's Name
    self.student_id = student_id              # Student's ID
    self.grades = []                          # Empty List to store grades
    self.grade_avg = 0.0                      # Initialize grade average to 0.0


 def add_grade(self, grade):
    self.grades.append(grade)                 # Add the new grade to student's grade list
    self.grade_avg = sum(self.grades) / len(self.grades)   # Update the student average
```

```
  def show_profile(self):
    print(f"Name: {self.name}")
    print(f"Student ID: {self.student_id}")
    print(f"Grades: {self.grades}")
    print(f"Grade Average: {self.grade_avg:.2f}")


# This is essentially the user-program portion

mary = Student("Mary", "S123")          # Add student by name and student_id
mary.add_grade(90)                      # Add grades in this fashion
mary.add_grade(95)
mary.show_profile()                     # Show the student's profile

gary = Student("Gary", "S889")
gary.add_grade(95)
gary.add_grade(97)
gary.show_profile()
```

Just for practice:

Add new students to the class, give them a few grades, and rerun the program. Make sure you understand how the "class" is being invoked or called, for example: name = Student("*name*", "*student_id*"), and then how each of the defined *methods* are called for the designated student.

Notes & Observations:

- In defining a class: The " __init__ ", is a *special method* used within Python classes. It is called automatically whenever an object of the class is created, and is used to *initialize* the attributes of the object.

- In the parameters that follow the " __init__ ", the parameter "***self***" is always the *first parameter*. It represents the object being created, such as "mary", "john", etc.

- Following the "self" parameter, add any *other parameters* that will be needed to pass and hold the information you desire for each object.

- For each student, "grades[ ]" is initialized as an *empty* list, and is populated whenever the program is executed and the "add_grade" method called.

- Continue to add a line, "*student_name.add_grade(score_val)",* for each new test score added into the average.

- For each student, a grade average is calculated every time the program is edited and executed. Whenever the "add_grade" method is called, it re-calculates the variable: "grade_avg", which will then show in the student's profile as an output.

- Note the use of the "f-string" method used in the print statements that are part of the "show_profile" method. Recall that this allows for a mix of datatypes – string, integer, and floating point, to be included within a "print" function.

Example 2:

In this 2nd example, we'll accomplish the same goal of creating a student roster that contains student profile information, a list of grades, and the student's current grade average. However; this will be a somewhat different approach; because in this example, both the "class" definition and what I'll call the "user-program", are saved as separate files. For this reason, the "class" will have to be "imported" by the "user-program" in order to build student objects. This is typical for larger projects, or where a greater degree of portability for additional users might be desired.

Here is the defined class and its respective methods, which is named: "student.py". As you can see; just like in our previous example, it is setup to handle student information (data), hold a list of all the student's grades, and calculate a current grade average. It is ready to be "called" by a user-program which will pass-along necessary data.

```
# student.py

class Student_Profile:
  def _init_(self, name, student_id):
    self.name = name
    self.student_id = student_id
    self.grades = []
    self.grade_avg = 0.0

  def add_grade(self, grade):
    self.grades.append(grade)
    self.grade_avg = sum(self.grades) / len(self.grades)

  def show_profile(self):
    print()
    print(f"Name: {self.name}")
    print(f"Student ID: {self.student_id}")
    print(f"Grades: {self.grades}")
    print(f"Grade Average: {self.grade_avg:.2f}")
    print()
```

Here is the user-program file, saved as "student_roster.py". Note that this and the class file need to reside in the same folder.

```
# student_roster.py

from student import Student_Profile     # Import the Student_Profile class from student.py

mary = Student_Profile("Mary", "S123") # Create a student and add grades.
mary.add_grade(90)
mary.add_grade(85)
mary.add_grade(95)
mary.show_profile()

bob = Student_Profile("Bob", "S456")   # Create another student and add grades.
bob.add_grade(88)
bob.add_grade(82)
bob.add_grade(91)
bob.show_profile()
```

Within this "student_roster" program, you can add new students, and add or edit grades. Each time you run the program, it will call the class "Student_Profile", providing updated output that reflects any additions or edits you've made.

Example 3:

In this 3rd variation of our example program, the program only allows grade entries for a *single* student. As you can see, all *flow-control* and the subsequent calls of other defined methods, are initiated from within the *main()* method that is defined within this class. This also shows some very useful keywords: the "sum", "try", "break", and "except" keywords, with comments on their usage.

```
Student_Grades.py
class Student:

  def _init_(self, name, student_id):    # Initialize the attributes of the object.
    self.name = name
    self.student_id = student_id
    self.grades = []

  def add_grade(self, grade):            # Add a daily grade to the student's record
    if 0 <= grade <= 100:
      self.grades.append(grade)
      return True
    else:
      print("Grade must be between 0 and 100")
      return False

  def calculate_average(self):           # Calculate the average of all grades
    if len(self.grades) == 0:
      return 0
    return sum(self.grades) / len(self.grades)      # Sum the elements within a "list" or "tuple".

  def display_info(self):                           # Display student information and grades
    avg = self.calculate_average()                  # Calls the "calculate_average()" method.
    print(f"\nStudent Name: {self.name}")
    print(f"Student ID: {self.student_id}")
    print(f"Daily Grades: {self.grades}")
    print(f"Number of grades: {len(self.grades)}")
    print(f"Average Grade: {avg:.2f}")
```

```
# main() is the method used to obtain student data (e.g. user-program).

def main():
  print("Enter student information:")
  name = input("Student Name: ")
  student_id = input("Student ID: ")
  student = Student(name, student_id)

  # Add grades
  while True:
    try:
      choice = input("\nWould you like to add a grade? (yes/no): ").lower()
      if choice == 'no':
        break
      elif choice == 'yes':
        grade = float(input("Enter grade (0-100): "))
        student.add_grade(grade)                    # Calls the "add_grade()" method.
      else:
        print("Please enter 'yes' or 'no'")
    except ValueError:
      print("Please enter a valid number for the grade")

  # Display student information
  student.display_info()                            # Calls the "display_info()" method.

if __name__ == "__main__":
  main()                                            # Calls the "main()" method.

# In Python, "__name__" is a built-in variable that evaluates to the name of the current module.
# When a Python script is executed directly, the __name__ variable is set to "__main__"
# This allows you to write code that only runs when the script is executed directly, rather than
imported as a module.
```

Notes on keywords:

- *sum*: Calculates the sum of the items within a list or tuple.

- *try*: Initiates a block of code where an exception may occur, but allow continuation of execution to the "except" keyword.

- *except*: Defines a block of code that executes when a specific exception occurs. It is partnered with the "try" block shown earlier in the code.

- *break*: Used to exit a loop (either "for" or "while") prematurely. Program execution continues at the first statement after the loop.

Modifications that may be useful for expanded capability and usefulness:

- Adding grade categories
- Including letter grade conversion
- Adding methods to remove or modify grades
- Saving data to a file
- Adding more student information fields

Create & Compile:

To compile your Python code into an executable file that can run on a computer without requiring a Python interpreter installed, you can use tools like PyInstaller, py2exe, or cx_Freeze. Here's a step-by-step guide for using PyInstaller, which is one of the most popular options:

Using PyInstaller

1. Install PyInstaller:

   First, ensure you have *pyinstaller* installed. It is installed using the manager utility called *pip* from the terminal window. If using VS-Code: go to "View" tab then select "Terminal". Key in the following:

   pip install pyinstaller

2. Run PyInstaller:

   Once pyinstaller is installed, use the following command in the terminal window to create an executable file from your python script.

   pyinstaller --onefile *my_script.py*

   - --onefile: Packages everything into a single executable file.
   - Replace *my_script.py* with the name of your Python file.
   - Note any messages that might indicate a problem in creating the executable file.

3. Locate the Executable:
   After PyInstaller finishes, you'll find the executable in the "dist" folder within your project directory.

   - On Windows: dist\my_script.exe
   - On macOS/Linux: dist/my_script

4. Test the Executable:
   Run the executable to ensure it works as expected:
   - Windows: Double-click the .exe or run it from the command line.
   - macOS/Linux: ./dist/my_script in the terminal.

Once compiled, you can distribute the executable to others, and they won't need the Python interpreter to run the program.

Example 4:

Here is one final variation of the *student roster & grade average* program shown in the previous section. There are many modifications that could be made that would add greater functionality to this program; such as saving our student lists to "file", adding additional student fields, and being able to print output for the entire student roster. This program, like the other examples, builds a student grade list and calculates the grade average of each student. It also prompts for user-inputs, allows for entering new student profiles, and adding grades to existing profiles. This is also a program that you could compile into an executable file using ***pyinstaller***.

```
Student_Roster_Grades.py
from student import Student_Profile                # Import the Student class from student.py

start_prog = input("Start Adding New Student profiles or Grades:  yes or no??\n").lower()
if start_prog == "yes":
   prog_active = True
else:
   prog_active = False
```

```
while prog_active is True:
    new_student = input("Would you like to create a NEW Student Profile: yes or no?\t").lower()

    if new_student == "yes":
        name=input("What is the student name?\t")
        student_id = input("What is the students ID number?\t")
        student = Student_Profile(name, student_id)
        continue_on = input(f"Would you like to add grades for this student? yes or no??\n").lower()
        while continue_on == "yes":
            new_grade = int(input("What is the new grade to enter?\t"))
            student.add_grade(new_grade)
            continue_on = input(f"Continue adding grades for this student? yes or no??\n").lower()
            if continue_on == "no":
                student.show_profile()

    elif new_student == "no":
        new_scores = input("Add grades for an existing student? yes or no?\t").lower()
        if new_scores == "yes":
            name=input("What is the student name?\t")
            student_id = input("What is the students ID number?\t")
            student = Student_Profile(name, student_id)
            continue_on = input(f"Are you ready to add grades for this student: yes or no??\n").lower()
            while continue_on == "yes":
                new_grade = int(input("What is the new grade to enter?\t"))
                student.add_grade(new_grade)
                continue_on = input(f"Continue adding grades for this student? yes or o??\n").lower()
                if continue_on == "no":
                    new_scores = "no"
                    student.show_profile()
        else:
            continue_prog = input("Would you like to EXIT the program:  yes or no? \t").lower()
            if continue_prog == "yes":
                prog_active = False
            else:
                prog_active = True
```

If you compile this program into an executable, you will essentially be left with a single file. Note that the co-dependent relationship between "Student_Roster_Grades.py", the user-program, and the defined class called "Student_Profile", still exists. Seeing that both of these ".py" files were in the *same folder when compiled*, the pyinstaller program recognizes the *import* statement and pulls the programming constructs from the "Student_Profile" class definition into the executable user-program. Again, the beauty of defining a "class" lies in its ability to be shared – providing tools, structures, and methods to other users and their respective user-programs. Take some time and inspect the "Student_Profile" code; imported from "student.py". Since it is used in all four examples, make sure you understand how the main user-program is calling the various methods, parameters and utilizing the list that is initiated from within the class definition.

Final Thoughts:

Python's strength and popularity lies not so much in its simplicity, but in its powerful performance for handling programming applications of all kinds. I hope you've gained a sense of what can be accomplished with Python, and know that you're not at the end of your Python journey. The skills you've gained here, and continue to gain as you apply them to your own projects are the foundation for a lifetime of exploration and mastery in programming.

Made in United States
Orlando, FL
04 November 2026

90204256R00057